So you <u>really</u> want to l

English
2nd Edition

Book Three

Answer Book

Susan Elkin

Series Editor: Nicholas Oulton M.A. (Oxon.)

GALORE PARK

www.galorepark.co.uk

Published by Galore Park Publishing Ltd
19/21 Sayers Lane, Tenterden, Kent TN30 6BW
www.galorepark.co.uk

Design and layout by Qué, Wittersham

Printed by Lego S.p.A., Italy

ISBN: 978 1 905735 69 3

First published 2006, new edition September 2012

Details of other Galore Park publications are available at
www.galorepark.co.uk

ISEB Revision Guides, publications and examination papers may also be
obtained from Galore Park.

Contents

Introduction

So you really want to learn English Book 3 Answer Book is intended for use both by teachers and parents and suggests answers to the exercises in *So you really want to learn English Book 3* where appropriate.

For some of the exercises, pupils will come up with a wide range of ideas and none of us can prescribe or predict what these will be. All an assisting adult needs to do is to encourage. Where I think it's appropriate and/or likely to be helpful, I have made suggestions, but these can be only examples of the sort of thing pupils might think of.

Each chapter of the pupil's book begins with three texts for comprehension: one fiction, one non-fiction and a poem. These are themed so that the subject matter shares some common ground across the three items.

Ideally a pupil should read through the text he or she is working on several times and have the opportunity to discuss it with a teacher before attempting the questions. It can help for a teacher to read the text aloud to the pupil first. Or, if he or she can read well enough, the pupil could read it aloud to the adult and/or the rest of the class. Then a second reading might be a silent one – although poetry with its close relationship to music is almost always better heard than read silently.

I have always found that, with a comprehension exercise, it makes sense to work through the questions orally with the pupil first and then set him/her the task of answering them independently in writing. Traditionally, comprehension answers are expressed in complete sentences which repeat part of the question because it reminds pupils of the essential features of a grammatically correct sentence. Some of the answers in this book have been slightly abbreviated.

I don't think we can remind ourselves too often that English is not Maths, or even Latin. Of course, there are some questions or items in exercises which have one irrefutable answer. But there are many more which do not – particularly when the question or 'answer' is a response to poetry.

Poets deliberately choose words or phrases for their ambiguity. They want the reader/listener to respond to the word in several different ways at different levels. In the poem 'November' by Ted Hughes (page 35) the words 'silvering', 'welding' and, 'hammered,' for example, all evoke scenes of a landscape which has been beaten into shape or moulded as if by industrial processes. Alert readers will spot and want to comment on more. That's the joy of poetry – but it also means there are few cut and dried answers.

Even in prose writing, often there are different words which mean something similar and many ways of expressing the same idea. That's fine. We want children to be original thinkers. So let's encourage them to think as broadly as possible in their answers and not be too absolute about right and wrong responses. We don't want to limit them.

It means, though, that quite often my suggested answers need to be mentally prefaced with phrases such as 'words to the effect of …' or 'something along the lines of …'. There will usually be other, equally appropriate, and perhaps better, ways of putting it.

And frequently pupils will think of something which I (or you) have not. It happens in the classroom all the time and should be encouraged. My answers are not necessarily definitive. Teachers, and others working with children, have to exercise a bit of humility sometimes. We don't know it all. Far from it.

Each chapter of the pupil's book has a spelling section because, of course, we all want the children in our charge to develop into accurate spellers. Remember, though, that it isn't a particularly useful skill to be able to spell a word aloud letter by letter. For many pupils, in fact, that's quite difficult to do because you have to visualise the word first which is a pretty sophisticated requirement. It is far more important (and generally easier) to learn to write down the words correctly spelt. So, when I teach spelling I always get the pupils to write rather than recite.

Teachers of English will have read many of the books I recommend in the 'Have you read?' sections. So will many parents, but I hope, in this third book, I have made some more suggestions which will be new to some adults as well as to children.

If you want to encourage a child to read there is no substitute for reading the same books and enthusiastically discussing that reading with the child. A child who sees respected adults absorbed in reading gets the message that reading is a grown-up, worthwhile activity and something to emulate. The worst thing an adult can tell a child in this context is that he or she is 'too busy to read'. That tells the child that reading is childish. So then, naturally, they see it as part of growing up to read less – or not at all.

But if you read books in parallel with 'your' pupil, whether you're a parent or a teacher, it becomes a shared experience, and very special and memorable. This could be yet another way in which parents at home can use *So you really want to learn English Book 3* to develop children's command of English.

Susan Elkin

Chapter 1

EXERCISE 1.1

1. Mrs Danvers must be a servant because she has made the bed and arranged the flowers. She is evidently quite senior in the household (not just a maid) since she has discussed the architecture of the house with the narrator.

2. (a)   wrapped, covered, shrouded

    (b)   swarthy, yellow, unwell

    (c)   initials, personal mark, name

3. She is Mrs de Winter because Rebecca was a de Winter and the narrator has married the same man.

4. The narrator is nervous and curious. She has gone exploring and opened the door because she wants to know what's there, but suffers a shock and panics momentarily ('For one desperate moment I thought that something had happened to my brain') when she sees Rebecca's things. She seems jealous of Rebecca and envies her glamorous possessions ('things I would have loved and almost worshipped had they been mine'). She wants to know more about her predecessor to such an extent that she smells and touches her nightdress in a faintly repellent way. Sometimes though she empathises with Rebecca. (For example, she understands why the other woman had used one hairbrush more than the other.)

5. Rebecca's apricot nightdress and her scents and powder suggest that she was more confident and more assertively feminine than the 'sallow and plain' narrator with her 'hair hanging lank and straight.' Rebecca's room is full of expensive possessions. So she was more flamboyant than the narrator who obviously does not have such things because she envies them and the glamour they represent. But Rebecca is 'in the crypt of the church with all the other dead de Winters'. So she is effectively a ghost in this passage. The narrator is frightened by Rebecca's presence because she can almost see, smell and hear her. Her legs tremble as she waits in vain for something to happen. Strangely, the dead Rebecca is stronger in this extract than the living narrator.

6. She is disturbed by the fact that the nightdress has not been laundered since Rebecca last wore it. She can see creases in it made by Rebecca's body and she can smell the remains of her scent. It makes Rebecca seem physically present.

EXERCISE 1.2

1. The first three stanzas are narrated by some sort of storyteller who questions the ailing knight-at-arms. From the fourth stanza we hear the knight's own account of what has happened to him. The poem is effectively a long question, followed by a detailed answer.

2. He has been entranced by a mysterious fairy woman – 'full beautiful.' He carried her on his horse to her 'elfin grot' where they made love and she wept. He fell asleep but when he awoke he was alone in the cold outside. He is now under a spell or curse because he is 'in thrall' and can never find peace, happiness or warmth.

3. He is desolate. His face is drawn and unhappy ('haggard and so woe-begone'). He cannot settle or come to terms with his loss. So with his shocked white face he just hovers ('palely loitering').

4. The birds have stopped singing. The grass on the lake has shrivelled and died. It is winter ('The squirrel's granary is full, / And the harvest's done') and it is cold on the hill's side.

5. (a) afflict, make you ill, upset you

   (b) horse, mount

   (c) bondage, slavery

   (d) wait, pass my days, linger

6. This is open ended. The possibilities include:

   'horrid': this word has a changed meaning; it had a much stronger meaning. Originally it was associated with horror.

   'sighed full sore': the alliterative sibilants ('s' and 'f') make it mysterious.

   'roots of relish sweet': there is an implication that she drugged him.

EXERCISE 1.3

1. They are highly mysterious because they seem to have been made and installed thousands of years ago by ancient people who, obviously, had no modern lifting gear. People puzzle about why there are so many and wonder what their purpose can have been. There is unlikely ever to be a definite answer.

2. (a) currents, waves, storms

   (b) system of lifting weights by raising them up with long rods or levers

   (c) invaded and took over government

3. Sweet potatoes were their staple food but these vegetables are not indigenous to Easter Island. Scientists do not know how they arrived on Easter Island from the Americas, the nearest part of which is over 2000 miles away.

4. The theory is that the long-eared people of Easter Island were the elite who ruled over the short-eared workers. It was the aristocracy who were commemorated in the statues.

5. Thor Heyerdahl knew that no one would believe that the Pacific Ocean could be crossed in the sort of small flimsy craft that the Polynesians would have had. So he built a replica raft and made the journey to show that it could be done.

6. The statues serve no practical purpose. Like medieval cathedrals in Europe, they would have required an enormous, collaborative labour effort to carve, transport and place in position. On the whole it is only religion which motivates human beings to such extreme endeavours.

7. It is thought that ropes were wrapped round the statue with a long length hanging from each side. The statue itself then functions as a pulley. One group of men hauls on one side. They are counterbalanced by a similar group on the other rope. If they haul alternately it would be possible to ease the statue a very short distance forward.

8. It is difficult to be sure of the age of the DNA which has been examined. Ancient Polynesians would not have left their DNA because their bodies were cremated after death, so the samples may instead be from a later set of Polynesians.

EXERCISE 1.6

1. Although he was frightened, because he did not understand what was happening, James opened the door firmly but quietly.

2. Did you really shout to frighten off any possible intruder as you entered the house, switched on the lights and noticed that something seemed to be wrong?

3. Sit up, shut up, listen and take plenty of notes!

4. In his novel *Bleak House*, Charles Dickens creates a character, Mr Krook, who dies through spontaneous combustion, an unexplained phenomenon which has long fascinated human beings.

5. All over the world there are statues in Catholic churches and cathedrals, usually of the Virgin Mary, which people say they have seen weeping real, physical tears, sometimes of blood.

6. Daphne du Maurier's best known novel dates from 1938 and, although she wrote many others, as well as some short stories and biographies, nothing ever touched the popularity of *Rebecca* except, possibly, *My Cousin Rachel*, which was published in 1951.

EXERCISE 1.7

1. antitheft
2. antepenultimate
3. antediluvian
4. antipodes
5. antenatal
6. anticyclone

EXERCISE 1.8

1. reliquaries
2. decoys
3. plutocracies
4. refectories
5. tercentenaries
6. forays

Sample sentences:

In Siena there are several reliquaries containing relics of various saints.

Because he wanted to deflect attack, the general left a few soldiers at base as a decoy to attract enemy fire away from the main body of men.

Since it is so easy to seize power if you have money, there are many countries around the world ruled by plutocracies.

Dinner was served in the refectory at 7pm each evening during our stay in the college.

The year 2006 was the tercentenary of the birth of Benjamin Franklin, who was born in 1706.

My grandmother has made various forays into language learning and at present is working hard at acquiring Polish.

Chapter 2

EXERCISE 2.1

1. She has retained tenure of two rooms – the bedroom and sitting room – of the larger house in which she lived before the sale. Once a lodger has been found for the sitting room she will, it seems, have only her bedroom.

2. Gunpowder and Pekoe

3. (a) assistant, helper, agent, representative (b) secretive, mysterious (c) goods for sale

4. The well scrubbed floor is covered with a piece of oil cloth in front of the table which is used as a counter – a mat for customers to stand on. The room smells and looks fresh because its walls have been re-plastered and painted white. The various blends of tea are stored in large boxes and decanted for sale into green containers. Also on sale are sweets for children. An official notice over the door declares Miss Matty's legal entitlement to sell tea.

    (Note: at this date it was against the law to sell tea, which was heavily taxed, without a licence – as with alcohol today.)

5. She (or he) is an observer who knows the town and its people well. She is kind to Miss Matty: she helps her get the shop ready and she has retained a small room in Miss Matty's former house (the rest of which is to be let) so that she can move in and look after Miss Matty if the latter is ill. She has a father who has firm ideas about how a business should be run – probably a successful man of business himself in Dumble which the narrator contrasts with Cranford.

6. Her furniture has been auctioned but someone – the narrator thinks it was Mrs Fitz-Adam – has bought Miss Matty's favourite things and given them back to her anonymously. The auctioneer and whoever advised the donor were part of this trick to save both Miss Matty's self respect and her furniture. Mr Johnson, an established grocer in the town, is kind when she tells him how anxious she is about setting up in competition. He even, behind the scenes, sends her some customers. The overall impression is of a community in which everyone knows everyone else and with a high level of tactful support for the less fortunate.

EXERCISE 2.2

1. The fruit is 'All ripe together'. Without cold storage different fruits would normally be available in different seasons.

2. 'Come buy' is repeated as part of the sales pressure. The words also add to the rhythm of the poem because they are single syllable ones, unlike faster moving words with several syllables such as 'cranberries' and 'pomegranates'. The poet was probably used to hearing traditional London street cries – the muffin man and the cats' meat man, for example – and based these words on their calls.

3. Buyers can enjoy the fruit with their sight ('Bright-fire-like'), with touch ('bloom-down-cheeked') and with taste ('sweet to tongue').

4. The short lines and rattling rhymes make the words tumble out very quickly. The fruits are listed and there's a lot of repetition of words ending in -berries which adds to the sense of urgency and speed. It's meant to make customers feel under pressure to buy.

EXERCISE 2.3

1. 'Voyage' suggests something much grander than a minor, local shopping trip because for the writer, looking back on his childhood, this first attempt to shop alone was a major event. It is almost comparing it with, for example, a voyage of discovery or a foray into war – an image he sustains with 'conquering hero' later in the passage.

2. He loses his sense of direction while crossing the green between the general store and the post office.

3. He doesn't want anyone to see that he is lost, or even out trying to manage alone or to offer to help him because it would be 'humiliating'.

4. White is using irony. Under normal circumstances walking hard ('slap bang') into a telephone box and bumping your head would be regarded as a misfortune. But he describes it as a 'stroke of luck' because it enabled him to get back on track without help from anyone else.

5. She shouts at Peter White as if he were deaf as well as blind. She refers to his mother rather patronisingly as 'Mummy' when he evidently calls her 'Mum'. She also draws attention to White's status as an errand boy for his mother rather than going along with the pretence that he's a grown up casually doing his own shopping.

6. Disabled children have to be taught how to look after themselves as independently as possible and it is one of the things social workers might try to help parents with because there is a natural tendency for mothers and fathers to be over-protective. But Mrs White has carefully worked out a strategy for herself. She has made him think that he is doing something very brave and possibly dangerous all by himself. In fact she has set the whole thing up to ensure that her son is completely safe. She has briefed the shopkeepers in advance but asked them not to help the boy unless something goes seriously wrong. And she follows him herself from a short distance – taking a short cut home when the shopping is finished so that he does not know. But she doesn't help him when he's lost on the green and lets him collide with the phone box. She is determined that he should learn how to do things for himself and knows that he will have to be allowed to make mistakes as part of the learning process. She doesn't need a social worker to tell her how to do any of this.

7. He is cheerful and funny, comparing the green in front of the shops with the Russian Steppes, for example. He can look back and laugh at himself, for instance, being greeted like a 'conquering hero'. On the other hand he is keen to explain to sighted readers just how difficult an experience like this is. He also shows affection and gratitude to his mother who evidently took such great care of him.

EXERCISE 2.6

Sample sentences:

1. I looked up.

2. He jumped over.

3. She looks well.

4. My brother tries hard.

5. I'll go later.

6. Because he was early for his appointment he had to wait around for half an hour.

EXERCISE 2.7

Suggestions only:

1. Before she wrote Cranford Elizabeth Gaskell wrote poetry.
2. We read 'Goblin Market' in class when we were in Year 7.
3. My mother finished the week's shopping after she had called at the school.
4. Once I have finished this exercise I shall have a rest.
5. Before they can play tennis Sam and Lucy will need their PE kit.
6. When public notices, leaflets and signs are prepared blind people's needs are usually considered.

EXERCISE 2.8

The following are examples only:

1. (a)   counterbalance – one object equalising another
           counterterrorism – activities preventing terrorist attacks
           countermand – to cancel

    (b)   transatlantic – crossing the Atlantic ocean
           transcript – written record
           transform – change

2. Words beginning with ab-:
    abort – end prematurely
    abnormal – unusual
    abridged – shortened

EXERCISE 2.9

1. theory or study of angels – angelology
2. great anxiety – angst
3. snake-like – anguine
4. x-ray photograph of blood vessels – angiogram
5. fisherman – angler
6. with sharp corners – angular

Chapter 3

EXERCISE 3.1

1. It must have been raining heavily because there is lots of mud in the streets. Horses, dogs and pedestrians are finding the roads and pavements slippery because of the water (presumably in puddles) and mud. Dense fog, worsened by the smoke from the chimneys, is making everything dark for the time of day. It is cold.

2. (a) clingingly, tightly, determinedly

    (b) rooms in private or charitable institutions for old people – like hospital wards. Dickens could also mean small areas, like mini 'villages', in towns which are called 'wards' for the purpose of local elections.

    (c) farmer, grower, food producer

3. Dickens mentions the Megalosaurus and describes it as an 'elephantine lizard' to emphasise just how muddy it is underfoot – as if we were in pre-historic times and the waters were just receding to form 'dry' land. Scientists were only just discovering the dinosaurs in Dickens's time so knowledge of pre-history was a novelty. It is also an exaggeration for emphasis – known as hyperbole. And it's a joke. The idea of meeting a Megalosaurus on Holborn Hill is incongruous and comic.

4. There are no mechanical vehicles – only transport drawn by blinkered horses. There are ships with rigging and other obsolete shipping such as collier-brigs bringing coal into London. The streets and shops are lit by gas not electricity.

5. 'Compound interest' is a banking term and therefore relates to the financial theme of the novel. (When you invest, say, £100 at 5% interest for a year your money is worth £105 after 12 months. That is simple interest. If you then leave your money, including the interest it has already earned, in the bank for a second year the interest will be calculated on £105. So at the end of the second year at 5% you will get £5.25 in interest because you have earned interest on your interest, as well as on the original £100 capital. That is called 'compound interest' because your interest is 'compounding' – building up – all the time.

    Dickens means that more mud sticks to the mud that is already there so it is building up like compound interest. It's an ideal metaphor for *Bleak House* which is about a long, unresolved legal case about the distribution of family money.)

6. He repeats the word 'fog' 13 times. The effect is both emphatic and humorous. You are left in no doubt that fog is the main concern of Londoners on this day. Repetition is generally avoided by writers because, used carelessly, it can be boring and lazy. Here Dickens is making a joke of deliberately pretending to be boring because fog is tiresome and tedious. More subtly, fog, which you can't see through, is a metaphor for all the misunderstandings which happen later in *Bleak House*.

EXERCISE 3.2

1. (a) The 'dragging grey columns' suggest rain falling thickly and heavily, straight down without the influence of sun or wind.

   (b) 'Glassy verticals' refers to rain so hard that it falls directly downwards and whose droplets are sharp looking and cold like pieces of glass. Both phrases indicate the relentlessness of the November rain.

2. He sees a tramp or vagrant, asleep and impervious to the heavy rain and 'welding cold'. The man is lying in water and getting wetter but he is wearing a coat and has each hand tucked into the opposite sleeve. He has wrapped pieces of sacking round his feet for extra warmth.

3. The pupil will choose but here are some possibilities, suggested as examples:

   'a seep silent all summer' is interesting because the alliteration (repeated 's') and long vowel sounds ('ee' in 'seep', 'i' in 'silent' and 'a' in 'all') evoke the quiet hissing, almost menacing, sound of the rain. 'Seep' has an assonant link with 'treed' in the previous line too.

   'welding cold' is effective because 'welding' suggests sticking together which is exactly what extreme cold does, for example, to fingers. It's a striking use of 'welding' also because the word is usually associated with heat and hot metal so it's really an oxymoron here. The two words are carefully chosen too for the rather chilling 'ld' sound which they share.

4. He sees a wooden frame (gibbet) on which a gamekeeper has hung the bodies of animals he has killed because they prey on game birds. They include weasels, cats and crows, owls and hawks. It's a rather sinister sight. Some have been there a long time and are now very stiff and papery ('weightless, twirled like dry bark bits'). Others are fresher and hanging rather defiantly in the rain. Gamekeepers used to do this in the belief that other animals would see it as a warning.

5. 'Treed' means covered with trees and 'gulleyed' means threaded through with little watercourses. In both cases the coinage (or neologism) is neat and succinct. Poetry is a very concise form. Hughes is able to convey in one word what it would otherwise take several words to do – and it would be much clumsier. The long, mournful sound of both words adds to the poem's dark atmosphere too.

6. The two poems share a title. Both are (partly) about the weather in November, the darkness and the lack of visible new life.

7. The Hughes poem is much longer and more serious than Hood's. It reflects on the ruthless beauty of nature even in extremes of cold and wet. Hood's poem is a light-hearted lament for the lack of all the things he enjoys at other times of year. The effectiveness of Hood's poem depends on a play on words because November happens to begin with the letters 'no'.

8. Hood has repeated the word 'no' (19 times) in just the same way as Dickens does with 'fog'. In both cases it's an ironic device to reinforce meaning.

EXERCISE 3.3

1. October was the eighth month in the Roman calendar, falling immediately before the ninth month, November.

2. The Anglo-Saxon word for November was *wind monath* or *blod monath*.

3. (a) dried up, withered, dead

   (b) to do with ghosts in a jokey upbeat way

   (c) associations, links

   (d) made the same everywhere and in all situations

4. All Saints' Day was a solemn day to remember and pray to saints. Today Hallowe'en involves 'fun and games' and is 'ghoulish' – which means it makes a lot of jokes about ghosts and creepy things rather than taking death seriously.

5. 5th November used to be a public holiday with church services, bell ringing and other ceremonies such as effigy burning. Today, apart from in places such as Lewes, it just means a bonfire party, perhaps with a guy, and fireworks.

6. It would coincide with the autumn half term which could then be in the same week for all schools. That would then be a good time for families to take time off together – and it might help them to feel more positive about the onset of winter.

EXERCISE 3.6

Suggestions only:

1. some/many/enjoyable/twenty

2. tiresome/winter/cold

3. quickly/in a thoughtful way/during break

4. born in the 18th century/a favourite of my father; fine/witty

5. few/most/more; modern/Elizabethan/19th century (and similar alternatives for the third gap)

6. most/many/more

7. some/cooked; tonight/tomorrow

8. no/more/great

9. his/my/Italian/good

10. their/your/rock; often/sometimes/much

EXERCISE 3.7

1. Thomas Hood's poems (p)
2. dos and don'ts (o)
3. novels written by Victorians (n)
4. St Mary's Church (p)
5. the reigns of Stuart Kings and Queens (n)
6. Queen Anne's reign (p)
7. six o'clock (o – was once 'of the clock')
8. the witness's statement (p)
9. we shouldn't (o)
10. the fox's habitat (p)
11. *Guys and Dolls* (n)
12. Aunt Glynis's house (p)

EXERCISE 3.8

1. I bought oranges, because they are my mother's favourite and she has a bad cold; bananas for Peter; some fresh dates, which we all like; unripe peaches, which will be ready in a few days and a big bag of overripe apples for my horse, who loves them for treats.

2. Our tour of America took us to New England where Dad was fascinated by Boston and its history; into California where we didn't like Los Angeles but loved the countryside; eastward along the Mexican border; eventually to Louisiana and Alabama and included highlights like Charleston in South Carolina.

3. This year Yasmin has already read three books by Charles Dickens, which she says she enjoyed very much; most of Daphne du Maurier, including *The Glass Blowers*; four modern crime novels; biographies of William Pitt and Charles Darwin and quite a lot of poetry.

EXERCISE 3.9

Sample sentences:

1. When we went to Delhi, my mother was keen to have a ride in a gharry although she was afraid that the driver might be ill-treating his horse.
2. In medieval Venice all Jews were forced to live in one area of the city, the ghetto.
3. Halloween is the night of the year when you are allowed to be as ghoulish as you like.
4. In Bombay, where the banks are steep, people access the Ganges via ghats.
5. There was a ghastly accident on the motorway last weekend.
6. As Queen Victoria's ghillie, John Brown served her and looked after her when she stayed in the Scottish highlands.
7. Some Indian food seems very oily because a great deal of ghee is used in the cooking.
8. When a small cucumber is pickled it becomes a gherkin.

EXERCISE 3.10

1. aggravate – provoke anger or reaction
   aggressive – confrontational or forceful posture
   arpeggio – notes of a chord played rapidly
   goggles – protective eyewear
   laggard – falling behind
   niggardliness – lack of generosity
   priggish – self-righteous
   smuggle – moving illegal goods
   toboggan – small vehicle on runners for use on snow and ice
2. A few examples: beggar, egghead, exaggerate, flagged, rugged.

EXERCISE 3.11

Suggestion only:

Fog everywhere.
Fog up the river, where it flows among
Green aits and meadows;
Fog down the river, where it rolls
Defiled among the tiers of shipping,
And the waterside pollutions of a
Great (and dirty) city.
Fog on the Essex marshes,
Fog on the Kentish heights.

Chapter 4

EXERCISE 4.1

1. Mr Slope has red greasy hair which covers his ears lankly and is firmly brushed stickily across the top of his head. His face is very flushed and his nose looks like a red cork. He has a large mouth with thin lips, protruding brown eyes and a domed forehead. He is tall with large feet and (clammy) hands.

2. The previous bishop's name was Grantly. He is dead ('late bishop'). The clergymen (prebendaries, minor canons, clerical doctors) were 'comfortable', 'happy, well-used, well-fed'. Bishop Grantly had 'kindly wings'. The implication is that these people have a shock coming to them.

3. Bishop Grantly's son was his chaplain. Mr Slope is now going 'to assume the station which had hitherto been filled by the son of the late bishop'. This too is clearly a big change.

4. Mr Slope means to take charge. He thinks he can become the dominant decision maker in Barchester although he's only the bishop's assistant. He plans to be the leader, control the money in the diocese and be admired by the poor.

5. (a) things, often part of the body, which stick out or protrude
    (b) carefully, accurately, correctly
    (c) roomy, spacious
    (d) clergymen attached to a cathedral chapter. He (or she in the 21st century) holds a prebend – a salary or piece of land. In the Church of England now 'prebendary' is sometimes an honorary title for a canon.

6. Trollope is building up an impression of a man who is very unattractive, but he is pretending to be even handed, so it's witty writing. He tells us mildly, for example, that Mr Slope's countenance (face) 'is not specially prepossessing' and then goes on to say his skin looks like bad beef and his nose like a spongy red cork. He uses the word 'intends' three times in the last paragraph to emphasise Mr Slope's ambitious determination to seize power in Barchester.

EXERCISE 4.2

1. The poem is narrated by the widowed Duke. He refers to his late wife as 'my last duchess'.

2. He is addressing a senior representative of a Count ('The Count your master'). He is prepared to marry the Count's daughter provided that there is a good dowry and that she and her father understand that she must obey her husband totally.

3. The Duchess has been murdered on her husband's orders ('I gave commands; / Then all smiles stopped') because he objected to the way she smiled at, and spoke to, the artist who painted her portrait and to other men in the court. The Duke is making this clear as a warning to the next possible Duchess and her family.

4. Suggestions only: 'Never to stoop', 'I gave commands', 'There she stands / As if alive.'

5. It shows that he collects very expensive art – just as he does wives. He expects them to obey him just as the seahorse is being forced to obey Neptune. It is an expression of the Duke's power. (Claus of Innsbruck is an imaginary sculptor.)

6.   Although the poem seems to flow fairly freely (in the same five beat rhythm that Shakespeare usually used) each line rhymes either with the previous or following one. This makes it seem very structured and formal. It is as if the Duke had planned very carefully in advance what he intended to say. It doesn't seem spontaneous. And that makes the warning even more menacing.

EXERCISE 4.3

1.   Jonathan Kent directed this production of *Sweeney Todd*.

2.   It was staged in Chichester.

3.   Suggestions only: nervous, spine-tingling, terror, demon, sinister, dark, rancorous, psychopathic, shrieking, nerve-fraying, darkness

4.   He objects to Jonathan Kent's having moved the setting from Victorian Britain to the 1930s. He regards such 'mucking about' as 'perverse' because the story is so firmly rooted in Victorian melodrama. Second, he is unimpressed by Michael Ball's casting in the title role. Although Ball looks sinister he doesn't quite – for Spencer – get to 'the dark rancorous heart' of Sweeney. Neither does he sing or act the part very well.

5.   We learn that Mrs Lovett is Todd's assistant and great admirer. Although she seems 'kind and cosy' it is her idea to put the victims' bodies into pies and feed them to customers.

6.   Charles Spencer wholeheartedly approves of Imelda Staunton's portrayal of Mrs Lovett. She brings 'wonderful comic zest' to it and 'gets superb value' from a clever, gruesome song about making a shepherd's pie with real shepherds. Not only is she better than Michael Ball but she is, Mr Spencer says, also much better than another actress, Lucy May Barber, whose role is 'feebly played and sung'.

EXERCISE 4.6

1., 4., 5. and 6. need altering. 2. and 3. are correct as they stand.

Possible answers:

1.   Always tasty at Pizza Express, lunch was enjoyable.

4.   With her dramatic voice, Fiona read the poem while the class listened.

5.   Falling on 14th February, St Valentine's Day is celebrated by lovers the world over.

6.   Inspired by Robert Browning, Andrew made it his goal to write a poem a day.

EXERCISE 4.7

1.   (a)   babies'   (f)   teachers'   (k)   armies'
       (b)   princesses'   (g)   headmistresses'   (l)   authors'
       (c)   ibexes'   (h)   bushes'   (m)   countries'
       (d)   churches'   (i)   scientists'   (n)   grandmothers'
       (e)   fairies'   (j)   musicians'   (o)   grannies'

2. Sample sentences:
   (a) The nursery floor was strewn with babies' toys.
   (b) Princesses' rights are being renegotiated in Japan.
   (c) Ibexes' trails were very clear as we began our safari walk.
   (d) Local churches' opening times are displayed in the library.
   (e) I used to imagine fairies' houses at the bottom of my garden.
   (f) Teachers' favourite time is break!
   (g) Mrs Ibbotson is attending a headmistresses' conference this week.
   (h) Bushes' shadows fell across the country path.
   (i) I like reading about scientists' discoveries.
   (j) The Musicians' Union is a well-established body.
   (k) Various armies' vehicles were on display at the international show.
   (l) Copyright law exists to protect authors' rights.
   (m) Countries' laws about drugs vary, but most are, rightly, pretty strict.
   (n) Grandmothers' memories were invited for the website.
   (o) Let's all ask for our grannies' thoughts.

EXERCISE 4.8

Sample sentences:

1. My bus pass is invalid so I must renew it.
   Although she has arthritis, her grandmother is determined not to become an invalid.

2. Every minute seemed to last an hour.
   Her brooch was minute but looked good on her small figure.

3. The second hand on my watch has stuck.
   Will you second my nomination for school council?

4. We often have to collect parcels from the post office.
   The Vicar said the collect for the day which, on Easter Sunday, is a beautiful prayer.

5. The pop star had signed a new recording contract.
   If hot metal cools it will contract.

6. *Reader's Digest* is my Grandpa's favourite publication.
   I cannot digest very fresh bread without getting tummy ache.

7. She has decided to learn the viola because she loves its mellow tone.
   The viola is a wild pansy.

8. James cried for a long time and his mother couldn't console him.
   Dad is very proud of his new console which includes a CD player along with DVD facility and radio.

9. 'I think I can rejoin the split in the wood', the cabinet maker told us.
   Amelia was inclined to rejoin rudely 'give over' or 'surely not' if she didn't agree with what we were saying.

10.   The official promised to process my passport application very quickly.

       On 14th July many people process though the streets of Paris to celebrate Bastille Day.

EXERCISE 4.9

Sample sentences:

1.   My older brother is known to frequent the library at university.

2.   The convict in *Great Expectations* is called Magwitch.

3.   I've always been a rebel because I don't like being told what to do.

4.   The president wanted to retire so he didn't contest the election.

5.   'Why did you absent yourselves from my lesson?' demanded the teacher.

6.   'Your conduct is unsatisfactory,' said Mr Jones with good reason because we'd wasted a lot of time in maths.

EXERCISE 4.10

1 and 2. air filled (e.g. a tyre) – pneumatic

          extinct flying reptile – pterodactyl

          poetic prayer, often sung – psalm

          doctor who treats mental illness – psychiatrist

          serious lung disease – pneumonia

          dropping of upper eye lid – ptosis

          skin disease – psoriasis

          false – pseudo

          study of ferns – pteridology

          government by the poor – ptochocracy

3.   The following are examples only:

      pseudonym – alias

      psychosomatic – physical illness caused by the mind

      Ptolemaic – relating to Ptolemy (either Greek astronomer or ruler of ancient Egypt)

EXERCISE 4.11

Sample answer:

Mr Slope is physically repugnant with his sweaty face and damp hands. He has large, ugly hands and feet, a red face and greasy, carrot-coloured hair. He is also unattractively vain and spends time styling his horrible hair. He is far too sure of himself and plans to show the people of Barchester how they should live. He is going to upset a lot of people.

EXERCISE 4.12

Sample answer:

I am willing to marry the Count's daughter but only on my own terms. I expect total obedience and require that my wife not so much as smile at another man, not even a portrait painter. If the Count's daughter becomes my wife and falls short of my expectations, I shall have her killed as I did my previous wife. I don't talk about these things or plead or offer second chances. I simply take action. Please make this clear to your employer and to his daughter.

Chapter 5

EXERCISE 5.1

1. North's translation of Plutarch is prose. Shakespeare has reworked it as poetry into his usual iambic pentameter and blank verse (five foot, unrhymed lines).

2. Cleopatra was sailing on the River Cydnus.

3. The vessel was rowed by a team of oarsmen using silver oars. They row to the rhythm of the music.

4. Shakespeare takes the royal colours, gold, silver and purple from Plutarch and the music which accompanies the rowing (although he cuts out the howboys, citherns and viols). He also adapts the comparison with the Roman goddess of love, Venus, and the attendance by the Cupid-like boys who are fanning Cleopatra. He amplifies these by adding the description of the fans ('divers-coloured') and an account of their effect on Cleopatra's 'delicate cheeks.' Other ideas added by Shakespeare include the image of the golden barge burning on the water and the suggestion that the water is in love with the oars and so follows them ('amorous of their strokes'). Generally, the Plutarch is more factual and the Shakespeare, unsurprisingly, more imaginative and dramatic.

5. (a) The sight of Cleopatra in her barge is so remarkable that no description can do it justice. It makes any attempt to describe it in words seem like a very poor thing in comparison.

   (b) The air movement created by the boys' fans is making Cleopatra's cheeks look pink and beautiful ('glow') so that the fans seem to be defeating their purpose of cooling her.

6. There is, of course, no correct answer to this. It's a matter of preference. Answers might comment on Shakespeare's use of poetry including his alliteration, imagery and compression of expression and/or on Plutarch's straightforward crispness. Remind pupils that the Shakespeare is part of a play whereas the Plutarch is a book to be read which makes a difference to style and impact.

EXERCISE 5.2

1. He has been watching them for 19 years ('The nineteenth autumn').

2. It is an autumn evening at dusk.

3. He has counted 59 swans.

4. The words 'clamorous' and 'bell-beat' describe the sound of the swans.

5. The narrator is fascinated by the symmetry and beauty of the swans rising out of the water as a group, quite suddenly, together. He finds beauty in their noisy, rhythmic circling in the air as they gather for flight. He thinks they are 'brilliant', which here is a precise word meaning brightly shining. And they are mysterious. He also comments on their pairing habits. Swans stay together for life and the narrator watches them 'lover by lover' being gently friendly ('companionable') as they swim about in the cold water or get ready to fly away. He admires the fact that 'Their hearts have not grown old'.

6. The mood is sad and wistful. Autumn is a sad time when everything is dying away or disappearing for the winter. So the narrator's 'heart is sore'. He, like the year, is ageing. He felt more cheerful and optimistic 19 years earlier when he 'Trod with a lighter tread'.

EXERCISE 5.3

1. (a) fancy, stuck up, showy, unnecessarily elaborate

    (b) like, similar to, a reminder of

    (c) cheek, sauce, daring, outrageousness

    (d) individuality, control of one's own affairs

2. (a) *soi-disant*

    (b) quasi-scientific

3. She blames the chemicals used by hairdressers. She includes perm lotions, neutralisers, colourings, mousses, gels, etc. She is also critical of driers, tongs and hot rollers.

4. Hairdressers sell 'treatments' to customers. These damage the hair, but hairdressers never admit this. Instead they pretend it is the customer's fault and offer more treatments to correct the damage – which makes it still worse. So it's a vicious circle.

5. She makes a case for simple washing with very little shampoo and, perhaps, conditioner. She says hair should be left to dry rather than be fast-dried with an electric drier.

6. She has grown her hair long so that she can manage it entirely herself. She wears it in a bun.

7. The 'value judgment' words include: pretentious, getting above themselves, servants, witches' brew, damaged, plethora, effrontery, hypocrisy, sanctimonious, conning, abuses, less than benign. (A case could also be made for others. For its length it is a highly judgmental piece.)

THE SEQUENCE OF TENSES

Pupils who study Latin will be familiar with the sequence of tenses which was, to the Romans, a very strict rule indeed. As we cover indirect speech in this chapter, and indirect questions in Chapter 6, it might be worth explaining the concept of sequence, which of course applies in English just as much as it did in Latin.

Essentially, tenses may be categorised as either primary or historic. The sequence of tenses dictates that if the main verb is primary, any subordinate verbs dependent on it must be primary too. Similarly, if the main verb is historic, the subordinate verb must be historic.

Primary tenses	Historic tenses
Present	Imperfect (was/were)
Future	Simple past
Perfect (with 'have')	Pluperfect (with 'had')
Future perfect ('will have')	

The complication arises when the direct speech (e.g. 'I am happy') is reported in a different tense to the direct speech itself.

Thus:

Direct speech: 'I am happy.'

Indirect speech:

She says that she is happy.

She will say that she is happy.

She was saying that she was happy.

She said that she was happy.

She has said that she is happy.

She will have said that she is happy.

She had said that she was happy.

Direct speech: 'I will be happy.'

Indirect speech:

She says that she will be happy.

She will say that she will be happy.

She has said that she will be happy.

She will have said that she will be happy.

She was saying that she would be happy.

She said that she would be happy.

She had said that she would be happy.

Direct speech: 'I have been happy.'

Indirect speech:

She says that she has been happy.

She will say that she has been happy.

She has said that she has been happy.

She will have said that she has been happy.

She was saying that she had been happy.

She said that she had been happy.

She had said that she had been happy.

Pupils will almost certainly find that they don't need to be taught this in this way, as it comes naturally, but a few may enjoy seeing the rule and comparing it with what they have learnt in Latin.

EXERCISE 5.6

Sample sentences:

1. Our English teacher told us that he had first seen *Antony and Cleopatra* at Chichester Festival Theatre in 1969.

2. Yeats thought the swans were mysterious and beautiful.

3. The poet John Keats believed that a thing of beauty was a joy for ever.

4. The Queen often includes her husband in the openings of her speeches.

5. The explorer asked his companion to lead.

6. My grandmother said that she had just read *Bleak House*.

EXERCISE 5.7

Sample sentences:

1. 'I have enjoyed playing Antony,' the actor told his friends.

2. 'I hope the new building will be finished by the beginning of next term,' said the headmaster.

3. Dr Carter declared, 'It is dangerous to whiten your teeth too often.'

4. 'Be as quiet as you can because Mum has a headache,' said Dad.

5. 'I have made plans to spend Christmas in Papua New Guinea this year,' announced Aunty Brenda.

6. Jamie explained, 'I want to go the supermarket on the way to Granny's so that I can buy her some chocolates.'

EXERCISE 5.8

Sample sentences:

1.   I shall wear my black-as-night dress to the ball.
2.   These one-size-fits-all socks are hopeless for me because my feet are so small.
3.   Open-for-business teachers were already waiting when we arrived at the parents' meeting.
4.   Professor Cassidy was one of those dry-as-dust speakers, unfortunately.
5.   Marie gave one of her fed-up-with-school shrugs and walked away.

EXERCISE 5.9

Parker – gamekeeper in a park
Chapman – trader
Cordwainer – leather worker
Wainwright – cart maker
Cooper – barrel maker
Palmer – pilgrim home from the Holy Land
Goldsmith – jeweller
Sawyer – a cutter of wood
Chandler – candle maker
Mercer – cloth merchant
Farrier – blacksmith

EXERCISE 5.10

Meanings and origins

1.   yuppie – person who is a young and upwardly mobile professional (semi acronym)
2.   technophobe – person who dislikes, or has a phobia about, computers and other technology (like claustrophobe)
3.   workaholic – person addicted to working (like alcoholic)
4.   cinephile – lover of films
5.   townscape – view of the city (from landscape)
6.   wordsmith – writer (a fashioner of words, like gunsmith)
7.   telethon – very long TV programme, usually for charity (from marathon)
8.   Oxfam – charity started in 1942: Oxford Fund for Famine Relief
9.   Ofsted – government body which inspects schools: Office for Standards in Education
10.   cyberspace – notional 'space' in which the internet works

EXERCISE 5.11

1. solemnity

2. columnist

3. autumnal

4. columnar

5. condemnation

EXERCISE 5.12

1 and 2.
    (a)   vigorous – energetic

    (b)   humorous – being amused or amusing

    (c)   glamorous – attractive and stylish

    (d)   clamorous – loud noise from a group of people

    (e)   rancorous – bitterness

Chapter 6

EXERCISE 6.1

1. The roofs of terraced buildings more than a hundred years old are best. Semi-detached and detached houses are separated by spaces too wide for the climber to cross and are therefore no good for people who want to climb across roofs. Twentieth and twenty-first century buildings tend to have steeper sloped roofs than older ones too which makes them difficult to negotiate. And modern TV aerials and satellite dishes are a nuisance. The more decorative features on the roof the better because elaborate chimney pots, and other features, make climbing easier by providing cover for the climber, but it is not a good idea to hold onto an old chimney stack which may be unstable.

2. A good roof climber is thin and supple with good night vision. He or she has no fear of heights although sometimes claustrophobics (people who fear enclosed spaces) make good roof climbers. Anyone who climbs roofs needs to be independent-minded and to want to be different from other people. Roof climbing attracts people who see their very dangerous 'hobby' (which most people would condemn as 'mad') as a way of finding freedom. They have a similar mentality to people who experiment with drugs or undertake a very challenging sport just to test their own reactions.

3. First, anyone seen on a roof by a passer-by will be assumed to be doing a legitimate rooftop job such as repairs to guttering. Second, anyone who hears footsteps on a high roof thinks that the sound must be something else because, for most people, roof walking is simply impossible.

4. (a)   roof tiles with an s-shaped cross section so that the downward curve of one tile overlaps the upward curve of the adjoining tile

    (b)   small building or structure protruding from the roof

    (c)   roofing with two slopes on both sides and both ends

5. Roof climbing is exhilarating. It is satisfying because it requires a lot of experience and skill to do it well. So, in a sense you can train in it and enjoy the sense that you are improving. It is liberating. Like skiers and white-water rafters, roof climbers get a 'buzz' out of the danger and the opportunity to push themselves to the limits – according to the narrator. But, of course, Vine is presenting the character as a very strange person. The reader can see that roof climbing is a totally unacceptable activity which no sane person would consider. So the deadpan, serious tone of this passage is really part of the characterisation – not a recommendation to go out and try roof climbing!

EXERCISE 6.2

Note: 'Lotos' was the standard 19th century spelling of a word usually now spelt 'lotus'.

1. The island is strangely sleepy ('weary dream'). The sailors can see a valley with the moon still above it. There are many streams but it's all uncannily calm and the water appears hardly to be moving – even where the streams reach the coast from cliff tops so that there ought to be waterfalls ('to fall and pause did seem'). What falling water there is looks like wisps of smoke drifting downwards. The sea around the island is calm ('slumberous sheet of foam'). The sun is shining on three mountains capped with old snow. Nothing seems to be changing or moving much.

2. They have given them each a taste of an extract of lotos, taken from the stem of the plant. This is a mood-altering drug and the sailors are immediately affected. Suddenly they no longer feel any urge to do anything (such as continue their voyage). Sounds seem remote, any activity is too much effort and all they want to do is to sit on the sand and dream pleasantly.

3. (a) without energy, spirit, interest or enthusiasm
   (b) foreign, strange
   (c) without life, dry, dead

4. You could pick almost any word in the poem. The long vowel sounds of strings of words like 'slow', 'veils', 'lawn', for example, work like slow mournful notes in a piece of music. The assonance of 'snow', 'clomb', and 'woven' has a similar effect. So do rhymes such as 'awake' and 'make' or internal rhymes such as 'deep-asleep'. He uses onomatopoeic lexis (lexis meaning the total stock of words in the language) to build an atmosphere of lethargy.

5. Each verse has nine lines rhyming ABABBCBCC. The effect of this is to create a sense of wandering because nine is not an even number and the rhyme pattern is asymmetrical. Of course, it's an illusion because the poem is highly structured. There is also a feeling that the poem starts and stops uncertainly because each verse ends with a rhyming couplet. The couplet acts like a full stop at the end of each verse. It brings the poem to a temporary halt. This mirrors the apathy and lack of purpose of the drugged sailors.

EXERCISE 6.3

1. He did not hand in the obligatory risk assessment paperwork before involving two pupils in a potentially dangerous activity.

2. If it is proved before the General Teaching Council for Wales that he has done what he is said to have done then he could be given a formal reprimand which would be recorded against him. He could also be temporarily or permanently prevented from teaching.

3. He was head of technology at Cefn Hengoed Community School in Swansea.

4. He took a sledge to school with him because there was snow on the ground. He showed it to a class of 15-year-olds as part of their revision and discussed with them how it was designed and how it worked. After the lesson two boys wanted to see the sledge in action so Mr Tremelling took them outside to a snowy slope where he demonstrated before letting them each try it under supervision.

5. They say that the rules are far too complicated and time consuming – the risk assessment for a school trip covers 12 pages. It would be better for schools to prepare just one shorter risk assessment document which could be used to cover all the activities a pupil might have to do while in school.

6. The headline makes light of the whole health and safety issue by dismissively imitating the way the headline writer thinks some officious, sloppily spoken people refer to it. All Mr Dolan's quotes are from people broadly in support of Mr Tremelling and others in a similar position. He does not, for example, quote anyone from Cefn Hengoed Community School such as the head teacher or the parent of one of the boys who sledged. Only the woman presenting the case at the General Teaching Council for Wales hearing puts the opposing point of view. Mr Dolan has, however, tried to get a statement from Mr Tremelling's union, National Assocation of Schoolmasters and Union of Women Teachers (NASUWT) but it could not comment while the case was in progress. This article is an example of mildly biased reporting.

DIRECT AND INDIRECT QUESTIONS

The sequence of tenses operates in indirect questions just as it does in indirect speech. You may wish to refer back to the primary and historic tenses discussed in Chapter 5 (page 73). The same principle applies, and pupils will see tenses change in the indirect question where the main verb introducing the question is in a historic tense.

Thus:

Direct question: 'Is she happy?'

Indirect question:

She asks whether she is happy.
She will ask whether she is happy.
She has asked whether she is happy.
She will have asked whether she is happy.

She was asking whether she was happy.
She asked whether she was happy.
She had asked whether she was happy.

Direct question: 'Will she be happy?'

Indirect question:

She asks whether she will be happy.
She will ask whether she will be happy.
She has asked whether she will be happy.
She will have asked whether she will be happy.

She was asking whether she would be happy.
She asked whether she would be happy.
She had asked whether she would be happy.

Direct question: 'Has she been happy?'

Indirect question:

She asks whether she has been happy.
She will ask whether she has been happy.
She has asked whether she has been happy.
She will have asked whether she has been happy.

She was asking whether she had been happy.
She asked whether she had been happy.
She had asked whether she had been happy.

EXERCISE 6.6

Suggestions only:

1.   When approached, my brother made it clear that he was both cross and busy.

2.   When the Italian Ambassador visited our school he asked why so little Italian is taught in Britain.

3.   Very politely, Mum asked me to lay the table for supper.

4.   Our history teacher asked us the date of the battle of Waterloo.

5.   Tom queried Alexander Fleming's discovery of penicillin because he thought it might have been Marie Curie.

6.   Ella went to consult the menu board because she wanted to know what was for lunch.

EXERCISE 6.7

Suggestions only:

1.   'Why aren't you in school uniform?' our form tutor asked us.

2.   'What time does the train leave?' enquired Peter.

3.   'Which car did you come in?' asked Granny.

4.   'Where is Newcastle?' Chloe demanded.

5.   'How many hours of prep do you have to do?' probed the school inspector.

6.   'Why didn't you vote?' the interviewer asked the Member of Parliament.

EXERCISE 6.8

Sample sentences:

1.   John's keenness to get onto the cricket pitch was obvious.

2.   Some pubs limit the number of drinks each customer may buy because drunkenness is so unpleasant.

3.   I like the openness of our tutorial sessions in which we can all say anything we wish.

4.   Some fashion models pursue thinness at the expense of their health.

5.   Once the orthodontist had finished with Jessica's teeth there was a new evenness in her smile which she was very pleased with.

6.   It is easy to mistake outspokenness for rudeness when a frank person often says things we'd rather not hear.

EXERCISE 6.9

1.   divers (as an adjective) – various

2.   groat – very small coin

3.   multitudes – crowds

4.   corse – dead body or corpse

5.   fain – rather not (e.g. I would fain not go)

6.   hie – go quickly

7.   twain – two

8.   verily – really (with the sense of 'in truth')

9.   sirrah – a way of addressing a servant or a child (we might say 'boy' today)

10.   chough – crow

Note: 'clefts' in 'The Lotos-Eaters' is related to modern words such as cleft (palate), cloven (hoof) and (meat) cleaver.

EXERCISE 6.10

1. 'How dare you flout the rules?' exclaimed the headmistress.

   Even if you're very well off it is bad manners to flaunt your wealth.

2. In a civil court of law the plaintiff is the person who brings the case.

   Even over the phone I could hear the hungry baby's plaintive cries.

3. My father is a deeply committed Jew but my mother is a religious sceptic.

   I put antiseptic on my cut to stop it going septic.

4. Fables like 'The Hare and the Tortoise' or parables like 'The Good Samaritan' have a moral message.

   The netball team's morale was raised by their win.

5. It is very easy to deprecate tabloid newspapers which carry a lot of trivial stories about celebrities, but some of them write well about health matters.

   A new car begins to depreciate in value as soon as you buy it and when it's a week old it will probably be worth a thousand pounds less than you paid for it.

EXERCISE 6.11

Suggestions only – this list is not exhaustive:

abductee, amputee, detainee, escapee, interviewee, licensee, lessee, returnee, trustee.

(Avoid words like jubilee, dungaree and fricassee which come from other languages and do not follow the same verb/noun pattern although they end in '-ee'.)

Chapter 7

EXERCISE 7.1

1. He was a compulsive gambler. It started with playing bridge during a holiday on the Isle of Wight and led, eventually, to debts which ruined him and left his widow with nothing.

2. She became pregnant while still a student. She refused either to settle down with the baby's father or to have the child adopted.

3. Her step-grandfather had been left sterile by mumps in puberty. Their marriage predated modern reproductive technology so there was nothing they could do.

4. She went to a caravan in Shropshire.

5. She is envious of Gran's age, experience and certainty. She is feeling very unsure of herself. For Gran, the sort of worries the narrator is coping with now are a long way behind her.

6. Gran is on holiday with her friend Beatrice. They are staying on the Pacific coast (probably in, for instance, California). The narrator imagines them drinking wine and smoking, perhaps something other than tobacco.

EXERCISE 7.2

1. Two are working away from home in the navy. Two more live away at Conway. Jane and John are dead. The little girl, who is speaking to the narrator, lives in the cottage next to the churchyard with her mother. That makes seven.

2. She insists that she is one of seven children, although two of her siblings are dead. That's why Wordsworth makes her tell the narrator four times that they are seven. It's repeated in the poem's title too.

3. The most striking thing is the simple language. It is mostly monosyllabic and there are few Latin-derived words. It makes the poem timeless (very close to the language of today) and emphasises the naturalness and certainty of the little girl.

4. She has thick, curly hair, pretty eyes and country beauty. Her clothes are 'wild' or very basic and unstylish. She is eight years old.

5. It is a religious poem because, for the little girl, death has not separated her from her brother and sister. As far as she is concerned they still exist (in heaven) and are still part of the family, although she understands that they are physically dead because she describes their deaths and burials. The narrator is admiring her faith and confidence and inviting the reader to do the same.

EXERCISE 7.3

1. A taboo subject is something which custom or convention does not allow to be openly discussed.

2. The writer's father was blind ('my father's blindness') so presumably his mother had to be his carer. But the implication is that his father was a difficult man. The disability wasn't talked about and Mrs Mortimer was generally regarded 'as a heroine and a saint' for 'putting up with' her husband.

3. She was teaching at Natal in South Africa, having studied art at college, when she was sent a newspaper cutting about her father's suicide.

4. She was an atheist. She had 'no use at all for God'.

5. (a) strong, impressive, indomitable
    (b) admired, worshipped, highly regarded

6. She was an individualist from Leamington Spa with artistic talent and a love of slightly risqué modern literature. She was a teacher. In her youth she rode horses bare back and swam in the nude. She rejected her mother's religion. In marriage she took on a difficult man who was (or became) blind. She cared for him with great devotion.

EXERCISE 7.6

1. Only we read 'We are seven' that morning. (No one else read it.)

2. We only read 'We are seven' that morning. (We didn't study it or learn it by heart.)

3. We read only 'We are seven' that morning. (We read nothing else.)

4. We read 'We are seven' only that morning. (We had read it very recently.)

5. *Turbulence* is the only novel by Jan Mark that I have read. (I haven't read any other novels by Jan Mark.)

6. *Turbulence* is the novel by Jan Mark that only I have read. (No one else has read it.)

7. *Turbulence* is the novel by Jan Mark that I have only read. (I haven't studied, discussed or reviewed it.)

EXERCISE 7.7

1. We must be sure to prepare for the exam carefully.

2. Are you ready to pay Gran a quick visit?

3. Mum told us that she used to like reading only books about horses.

4. I really will try to practise the trumpet regularly.

5. Let's get ready to have a really enjoyable time.

6. Americans often like to use split infinitives.

EXERCISE 7.8

Sample sentences:

1. Fancy! Cauliflower cheese for supper.
    Fancy cauliflower cheese for supper?

2. Can you wait a minute while I wash, Claire?
    Can you wait a minute while I wash Claire?

3. This painter claims John Mortimer, the famous playwright, is outstanding.
    'This painter,' claims John Mortimer, the famous playwright, 'is outstanding.'

4. 'Let me introduce you to Sophie, Ellis.'

    'Let me introduce you to Sophie Ellis.'

5. John said my friend, Paul, is a fine cellist.

    'John,' said my friend Paul 'is a fine cellist.'

EXERCISE 7.9

1. monologue – performance by a single speaker
2. bibliomania – obsession with books and reading
3. monogamy – marriage to a single partner
4. monochrome – black and white
5. trichotillomania – obsession with pulling out one's own hair
6. monolingual – able to speak only one language
7. monosyllable – a word with only one syllable
8. pyromania – obsession with fire

EXERCISE 7.10

Sample sentences:

1. If you grow irises you need to dig up their knotted rhizomes and divide them every four years.
2. Our teacher is an individualist, but that's what makes her so charismatic and why we learn such a lot with her.
3. Brahms wrote a beautiful rhapsody for contralto soloist, male choir and orchestra.
4. I tend to confuse geometric figures with four angles and sides so I have to work hard to remember that the rhombus is the one which is like a square pushed sideways.
5. Rufus didn't get a solo part in *Annie* but he thoroughly enjoyed singing in the chorus.
6. Because my neighbour has severe arthritis she cannot bend down to attend to her feet so she goes to a chiropodist.
7. Chemotherapy is drug treatment for cancer and it saves many lives.
8. The swimming pool I use now has a new filtration system so it needs less chlorine to disinfect it.

Chapter 8

1.   The animals had been fighting a battle against invaders of their farm – a skirmish known thereafter as 'The Battle of the Windmill'. It has led to the destruction of the windmill and two years' painstaking work. Some of the animals have been killed in the fighting and others are injured.

2.   Squealer did not fight on the front line. He has saved himself by keeping out of the way. The ordinary animals have not realised that this was an act of self-interest or cowardice but they are puzzled. Orwell lets the reader see 'past' the animals' reaction so that we know the truth.

3.   Napoleon is the top leader. He uses ceremony to impress the animals. He walks at the front of the funeral procession and takes credit for the 'victory' (which was really a defeat) by creating a new honour and awarding it to himself. But he knows how to placate the ordinary animals who aren't very intelligent. He arranges for a tiny gift for each of them so that they all think they've been treated well and rewarded.

4.   Boxer is a very strong worker and brave fighter. He has been injured in the battle. When he thinks about rebuilding the windmill he tries not to be disillusioned, but fears his strength might be lessening. Unlike Squealer he knows just how much physical effort it will take to re-build the windmill. He has common sense. That's why he asks about the gun and the 'victory'.

5.   It is to suggest that they are all equal although clearly they are not. 'Comrade' was how Russians addressed each other after the Russian Revolution and the end of the Russian royal family in 1917.

6.   The animals are governing themselves without human beings so this passage is about government. It's also about how some animals, or people, will always seize power – as Squealer and Napoleon have done – under any circumstances. The leaders are manipulating the others by getting them to fight for them and by not telling them the truth. To argue that the loss of the windmill is a victory is absurd but Squealer persuades the others. The piece (like the novel that it comes from) is a satire about the workings of human government. The animals and the farm are an allegory.

1.   He imagines them sleeping well despite their poverty and uncomfortable surroundings. He wishes he could sleep too.

2.   He is speaking to a personification of sleep ('O sleep, O gentle sleep'). He imagines sleep as a kind visitor who calls on people in their beds to 'seal' them into 'repose'.

3.   The synonyms for bed(s) are: cribs, pallets, canopies, couch and cradle.

4.   Even the ship-boy, who has to rest high up on a 'high and giddy mast' out at sea where it's noisy ('deafing clamour') and rough ('rude imperious surge') is able to get to sleep. So it seems very unfair that the King in all his comfortable luxury ('appliances and means') cannot.

5.   Possible answers:

      'Nature's soft nurse' uses a combination of soft 'n' and 'f' sounds with the hissing sibilance of the three uses of 's' to evoke a soothing sound. It suggests that sleep is a gentle caring companion.

'leavest the kingly couch / A watch-case or a common 'larum-bell?' is an example of alliteration being used to emphasise the speaker's point. The repeated 'c' and 'k' sounds connect the high 'kingly couch' with the low 'watch-case' and 'common' – a continuation of the speaker's contrast between himself and his subjects who are beneath him in rank.

6.   He thinks that it is because he is King and has so many worries that he cannot get to sleep. He thinks that life is easier and more carefree for his subjects. The crown here symbolises his kingship. This line is a summary of everything he has said in this speech.

EXERCISE 8.3

1.   The spelling of 'honor' and 'program' indicate that the writer is American.

2.   Passage B contains many references to events in Britain triggered by Gaddafi's regime such as the Lockerbie crash, the death of WPC Yvonne Fletcher, the 1984 bombings and the death of the Libyan journalist in London. These are events the writer expects readers to remember and be interested in.

3.   Gadaffi was either 26 or 27 (depending on which month he was born in) when his rule started. (He was born in 1942 and became leader in 1969.)

4.   There are plenty to choose from! For example, Passage A: inspiration, unique, defiant, warrior-king, honor, welfare, martyrdom, goons, martyred. Passage B: dictator, subjugation, terrorism, erratic, vain, unpredictable, self-styled, tyrants, hell-bent, murder, mayhem, mass murder, ruthlessly liquidated.

5.   (a)   Passage A praises Gaddafi for leading international groups in their hostility to Western causes. It also applauds his personal bravery and his humane approach to spending money on his people at home.

     (b)   Firmly describing Gaddafi as a ruthless dictator, Passage B draws attention to the many terrorist attacks instigated or supported across the world by his regime. It also ridicules his excesses.

6.   The writer wants to show how eccentric and unpredictable Gadaffi was – as well as hinting that surely a man who behaved like this couldn't really have been a fit and responsible ruler. The outlandish arrangements would, apart from anything else, have been almost unimaginably expensive – money another ruler might have spent on something more worthwhile for his people. It is also a way of poking fun at Gaddafi although the writer quickly points out that most of what Gaddafi did was certainly not a joke.

7.   According to Passage A Gaddafi was an exceptionally courageous man who 'fought to the death' at the end of his life. And, rather than spending money on weapons, he supported education projects. He was involved in and/or leader of the international groups listed in the first paragraph.

8.   Among other things Passage B describes the 1988 bombing by Libyans of a passenger aircraft over Lockerbie as 'the biggest mass murder in British history'. It also roundly condemns Gaddafi for supplying terrorist organisations such as the IRA with arms.

9.   One rather hopes most users of *So you really want to learn English Book 3* will plump for Passage B and explain their reasons articulately but, of course, we must keep an open mind…

     Passage A uses very emotive, fulsome language to praise Gaddafi and few opportunities are missed to include an upbeat adjective – e.g. unique, defiant. It also refers to him as an inspiration and mentions martyrdom. At the same time it is heavily critical of the West – referring to arrogance, usurpers, goons and aggression. It completely ignores many of the facts about Gaddafi mentioned in Passage B. It stresses what it sees as Gaddafi's virtues and achievements such as spending money on education for his people. It is a pretty shallow, transparent piece of propaganda.

Passage B, on the other hand, is more measured and less emotive as if the writer thinks that the facts mostly speak for themselves – although the words 'subjugation' and 'terrorism' both appear in the first paragraph. The writer uses wry (typically British) humour to ridicule Gaddafi with the account of his eccentric behaviour (brunettes with machine guns, camels at summit meeting etc.). The piece also stresses his extravagance which Passage A plays down. It then goes on to detail the very serious incidents blamed on Gaddafi such as the Lockerbie bombing and the shooting of a policewoman in London, neither of which is mentioned in Passage A. Most of this – and the other incidents mentioned – is recounted in fairly plain factual language e.g. 'One Libyan journalist opposed to Gaddafi's regime was assassinated as he walked past London's Regent's Park Mosque.'

It could be useful, when studying the nature of propaganda to get pupils to discuss the connotations of words which mean killed such as: assassinated, shot, martyred, blown up, slaughtered, executed, despatched, butchered.

And/or pose for discussion the question: What is the difference between a terrorist and a freedom fighter?

It depends, of course, which side you're on.

EXERCISE 8.6

1. George Orwell wrote <u>fewer</u> books than Charles Dickens.
2. Do we need more or <u>fewer</u> suitcases for this year's holiday?
3. We have <u>less</u> luggage than usual.
4. In the end Gadaffi had <u>fewer</u> supporters than he needed in Libya.
5. This queue is for shoppers with <u>fewer</u> than eight items to pay for.
6. There is <u>less</u> traffic on the M25 after about eight o'clock.
7. I am trying to eat <u>less</u>.
8. That means I munch <u>fewer</u> chocolate bars.

EXERCISE 8.7

1. 'Please don't <u>lie</u> to me,' said the headmaster.
2. Let's <u>lie</u> on the beach and rest for a while.
3. The old man had <u>lain</u> on the floor for an hour before he was found.
4. Our new carpet was very well <u>laid</u>.
5. 'Let us <u>lay</u> these <u>lies</u> to rest,' said the policeman, trying to get at the truth.
6. Black Colombian hens <u>lay</u> the best eggs.
7. 'I don't enjoy a <u>lie-in</u>,' <u>lied</u> Thomas.
8. While the twins <u>lay</u> on the sofa resting, Mum <u>laid</u> out their party clothes.

EXERCISE 8.8

1. I want to re-read *Henry IV part 1*.

2. Muammar Gaddafi was never chosen as the ruler of Libya.

3. After the Battle of the Windmill, the animals were also very tired.

4. I shall change my library books later.

5. All formal invitations should be replied to.

6. Before exams it's a good idea to revise your work.

EXERCISE 8.9

1. Years passed. The seasons came and went. The short animal lives fled by. A time came when there was no one who remembered the old days before the rebellion except Clover, Benjamin, Moses the raven and a number of pigs.

   (From *Animal Farm* by George Orwell)

2. The letter from Guy was still on the desk where I had left it. Wondering why I had bothered to keep it once I had read it, I tore it up and dropped the pieces in our waste bin.

   Silver, watching me, said, 'Are you going to?'

   'Am I going to what?'

   'Marry him. This guy, Guy.'

   I could hardly believe it. I stared at him. 'Of course I'm not going to marry him. I'm too young to get married.'

   (From *Grasshopper* by Barbara Vine)

3. Oz is a big bloke and I am not small but it took our combined weight to shift whatever was behind the door far enough for Oz to squeeze through. I stayed outside and put my hand round it. Sandor was collapsed on the floor between the wash-hand basin at one end and the lavatory at the other, half sitting against the door, feet against the opposite wall. I couldn't see his face. He didn't seem to be breathing.

   'Is he dead?' I could only whisper it.

   (From *Turbulence* by Jan Mark)

EXERCISE 8.10

1. Although the word 'awesome' is often misused it really does describe accurately most people's reaction to the Pyramids.

2. Midges can be very bothersome in Scotland although some people are unaffected.

3. Traffic noise is tiresome when it continues all night.

4. Wholesome food includes fruit, vegetables and home cooked dishes.

5. Mr Jones's comments about my painting were so fulsome and complimentary that I didn't really believe him.

6. Boxer and the other animals on Manor Farm found the rebuilding work irksome.

EXERCISE 8.11

1. quarrelsome – argumentative
2. winsome – charming, engaging, winning
3. venturesome – adventurous, outgoing
4. meddlesome – given to interfering
5. noisesome – loud, noisy
6. wearisome – tiring, tedious

Chapter 9

EXERCISE 9.1

1. (a) unhurt, untouched, unaffected

    (b) impossible to get into or break up

    (c) change sound or pitch like a piece of music moving into another key

2. Stephen has been shot in the neck by a bullet from a rifle and he has a piece of flying metal (shrapnel) buried in his shoulder. The blast has knocked him out and he is suffering from concussion. More superficially there are many tiny metal fragments in the skin of his dirty face.

3. It was a whole day before Byrne and Hunt and the stretcher bearers could get Stephen to a dressing station. The men were under attack and the rule was that they must first keep building up the defences and second help the injured who were able to walk. Men with serious injuries who needed to be carried had to wait. It didn't help either that one of the dressing stations had been destroyed by enemy action. By the time Stephen reached a dressing station it was 30 hours since his injury.

4. He is delirious first because of a fever caused by infection in his injuries and then because the seriousness of his condition is making him drift in and out of consciousness. His mind leaps from place to place and different times of his life. He thinks of the orphanage he grew up in and believes he is there. He imagines he's in a house in France with a woman called Isabelle. He half-dreams, half-thinks of his school. He feels angry and unloved. He screams for his mother (who presumably either died or abandoned him if he was an orphanage child).

5. No, he won't die although he is almost at the point of death when they put him out in the rain to wait for transport to the temporary hospital. While he is waiting he reaches a turning point in what is really a 'near death experience'. He imagines he hears a voice urging him not to give in (to death) for the sake of the 'peace he longed for'. That would be the easy option. He has to make 'the effort of courage' and return to the messiness of life to have some more experiences. The writer wouldn't tell us all of this if the man then died.

EXERCISE 9.2

1. The drowning man, who doesn't get his gas helmet on quickly enough, is a victim of chemical warfare. He is being choked by poison gas which has been hurled across in capsules by the enemy. It surrounds the men in green clouds like water so, as he falls it is as if the 'guttering, choking' man is drowning.

2. There is a lot of mud. Some have lost their boots. They are exhausted ('Drunk with fatigue') and very frightened. Some are injured and they are trying to get away from poison gas. It is not surprising that they are 'Bent double' and 'Knock-kneed' or that they can only 'trudge'.

3. It was a traditional rallying cry as governments, senior officers and even family at home assured young troops that they were doing something noble by fighting for their country. In the 1914–18 war, the physical reality of front line fighting and the very high casualty rates meant that it was anything but sweet and right. Owen, who died in action in 1918, is suggesting that anyone who quotes or believes the tag hasn't been in the front line.

4. There are many options. For example:

'Obscene as cancer' compares the devastating effects of poison gas on the human body with the ravages of cancer. The difference is that cancer develops randomly. The gas is deliberately inflicted by one group of human beings on another. It is striking, too, that the man is dead (on 'the wagon we flung him in') but the gas and its effects are still alive 'gargling from froth-corrupted lungs'.

'blood-shod' means that their feet are bleeding so badly that it is as if they are wearing shoes made of blood. The two short vowel sounds each followed by a 'd' creates a half rhyme and – onomatopoeically – a slow, dead plodding sound like their trudging. With 'limped on' which precedes 'blood-shod', the poet also uses the four syllables to suggest the rhythm of a loud human heartbeat as the men try to get away.

5. The rhyme gives the horror of the action inevitability because you listen for the next rhyme and so it pushes the poem forward. The first fourteen lines of the poem are, effectively, a sonnet with an octave and a sestet with alternate lines rhyming until the shock of 'light' and 'drowning'. After that it's less regular and more jagged as the narrator moves on from describing events to reflect on how he is haunted by his memories of the gas-poisoned man and the immorality of sending innocent people to exist in these conditions. He links the quasi-sonnet with the rest by repeating the word 'drowning'. Most lines have three or four beats but the rhythm is jerky to evoke the danger and uncertainty of the situation. The occasional short line emphasises this effect.

EXERCISE 9.3

1. He is trying to be factually very accurate. This is not fiction. He is trawling his memory for every fact he can recall. In 1916 very few people in Britain would have travelled abroad so, in one sense, it was a novelty for a young man to be in France. But, by the late 1960s, when this memoir was written many people were beginning to travel in Europe on holiday. So the writer perhaps thinks that some of these names may, by now, be familiar to the members of his family for whom he is writing.

2. He was hurt so badly that he had to be taken away from the fighting and brought back to Britain for treatment and to recover. If he had stayed in the front line he would almost certainly have been killed as many young soldiers in the Somme Offensive were (almost 60,000 British casualties on the first day alone).

3. He has to get help for anyone who, like William Hillyer, is injured. His job is also to catch and send back anyone who is losing his nerve and trying to slink away from the terrors of the front line: the so-called 'cowards'.

4. Their commanding officer knew that many of the men would be killed. He therefore makes sure that the soldiers get a bit of pleasure from reading their letters and talking to their friends because they may never get another chance. It is a form of kindness in a very harsh situation.

5. His foot was clearly very badly hurt. He needed emergency surgery and, later, many operations to remove pieces of 'diseased bone'. Immediately after the injury he was probably faint with the pain and in and out of consciousness. He may also have had an infection resulting from the wound, in which case fever would have made him delirious. And the doctors may have given him a strong pain killer, such as morphine, which would have made him sleepy and inclined to lose track of time.

EXERCISE 9.6

Suggestions only:

1. I have… walked, researched (the topic), circulated, acted (a role), wandered, composed (a song), tidied (the kitchen), worked, talked, carried (the argument), begged (him), played (football), cried, laughed, shouted, cooked (breakfast), combed (my hair), danced, closed (the door), waved.

2. He has… spoken, thought, sung, drunk (his water), bought (a car), sat, swum (a length), lain, struck (a bargain), driven (her car), woven (a mat), brought (his mother), written, made (a cake), gone, broken (the vase), run, read (the book), got (a horse), flown (an aircraft).

EXERCISE 9.7

1. It should read: Verbs have to agree with their subjects. The word 'has' is an example of a verb not agreeing with the subject.

2. It should read: Prepositions are not words with which sentences should end. His sentence, which ends with 'with', demonstrates the inelegance of ending with a preposition although sometimes it's unavoidable. (Winston Churchill once joked 'Up with which I will not put' to show how clumsy slavish avoidance of prepositions at the end of sentences can be.)

3. 'And' is a conjunction and he's started his sentence with it. Many writers – Dickens for example – do this all the time. Remember the beauty of the 1611 Bible too. But (I do it too!) pupils need to be aware of the danger and avoid doing it too often or by mistake.

4. Should read: It is wrong to split an infinitive – ever. Or better still: It is always wrong to split an infinitive. 'To split' is an infinitive and he has split it with an adverb 'ever'. Avoidance is recommended where possible, but as with point 2, it is sometimes the only way without resorting to clumsiness.

5. A cliché is an overused expression. 'Like the plague' is an example.

6. Alliteration is the repetition of the same letter or sound, usually at the beginning of neighbouring words, for literary, visual or comic effect but it can be irritating. In the editor's sentence all the words begin with 'a'.

7. If you are being specific you would not use a vague expression like 'more or less.' You should say precisely what you mean.

8. Parenthesis means brackets. Much of what is casually put in brackets is unnecessary. There are two examples in the provided sentence. Neither adds much.

9. To be formally grammatical every sentence should have a finite verb. Without one it isn't technically a sentence. It's a fragment like: No sentence fragments. As with point 3 pupils should be wary of this but, like many great writers, they will want to use fragments deliberately sometimes. What fragment users are actually doing is to use an established spoken form in writing – for all sorts of reasons.

10. This is similar to point 7. Say what you mean with examples. Avoid the use of 'one' because it usually indicates that there is an unsubstantiated generalisation coming.

EXERCISE 9.8

Suggestions only:

1. The diversion on the M11 turned all the traffic off the motorway and meant we had to go a long way round to get to Stansted Airport.

2. My sister and I are very outgoing but my brother is more of an introvert.

3. I don't usually mind heights but when I reached the top of the London Eye everything started to turn as I succumbed to a nasty attack of vertigo.

4. Our English teacher is inclined to subvert the discussion if she thinks we're getting too far away from the point.

5. He drew a transverse section of a plant stem to show us how it looked if turned sideways.

6. The Liverpool versus Arsenal match was very exciting because it makes good football to see two such evenly matched teams turned against each other.

EXERCISE 9.9

1. British industry has moved away from manufacturing toward saleable services.

2. Because decorated fingernails are so fashionable my hairdresser now also works as a manicurist.

3. There were a lot of delays during the building but our school's new swimming pool is now operational.

4. Manoeuvring the car round the bend into our garage takes great skill and a lot of practice.

5. Each piece of music a composer publishes is given an opus number to distinguish it from his or her other works.

6. If you try too hard to get other people to do what you want you will be accused of being manipulative.

Chapter 10

EXERCISE 10.1

1.   (a)   Miss Maria Ward

       (b)   Miss Frances (Fanny) Ward

2.   Frances Ward married what her family regarded as a common sailor, 'a Lieutenant of Marines'. He was 'without education, without fortune, or connections'. This was hard for her sisters, one of whom had married a rich baronet and the other a clergyman working for his wife's brother-in-law. It was an 'untoward choice' and an 'imprudent marriage' which her elder sisters thought she had decided on to 'disoblige her family'. Frances Ward didn't tell her sisters about it until she was already married. For a long time the two elder sisters had no contact with the younger.

3.   She married Sir Thomas's clergyman friend because it gave her a comfortable living of £1,000 a year (the equivalent of at least £100,000 in today's money). She thinks she has a right to tell her sister how she should live her life. She writes 'a long and angry' letter which upsets Mrs Price so that they don't speak for a long time. She seems to be self-opinionated and bossy.

4.   Maria Ward had a dowry of £7,000 (at least £700,000 today). Her uncle is surprised that Sir Thomas Bertram was prepared to marry her with less than £10,000. He thought she was 'at least three thousand pounds short'.

5.   It mentions money repeatedly. It comments on Maria Ward's dowry and Sir Thomas's 'large income'. It tells us about Mr and Mrs Norris's £1,000 a year and that Mr Price was 'without fortune'. It is a pragmatic, practical, even cynical, approach to the economic realities of marriage. Love is not mentioned.

6.   (a)   superior status

       (b)   hesitate

       (c)   protest

       (d)   communication

EXERCISE 10.2

1.   (a)   If love changes then it is not genuine love.

       (b)   Love is not something which becomes jokey as time passes. The image is of love as a master of, say, a Jacobean household and Time as his paid 'fool' or joke-maker attacking his master with his wit.

2.   Love is mentioned five times in 14 lines. The narrator of the sonnet (unlike Jane Austen 200 years later, perhaps) is suggesting that undying love is the basis of a good marriage.

3.   If 'true' minds – that is minds which are faithful to each other – marry, then nothing can stop them having a good marriage. Real love does not change when other things change. It will triumph over death and last until 'the edge of doom'. It's a very confident and attractive assertion of the power of enduring love – which is why it has long been one of the most popular of Shakespeare's 154 sonnets.

4. I shan't be proved wrong (about the strength of lasting love). I stake all my writing and my experience as a man on it. It's effective because it's a complex message expressed very simply and directly in two lines which are almost monosyllabic. That makes sure that the couplet hammers its message home syllable by syllable. The double rhyme acts like a stopper at the end of the sonnet.

5. Love is not weak with superficial beauty such as flushed cheeks and a pretty mouth. He is strong and cannot be hacked down by Time trying to cut him back like a crop at harvest time with his 'bending sickle'.

EXERCISE 10.3

1. (a) Dr Robert Epstein is an academic (lecturer/researcher) at Harvard University (Boston, USA)

    (b) Francine Kaye wrote *The Divorce Doctor*.

2. Indian, Pakistani and Orthodox Jewish communities favour arranged marriage.

3. He has studied love and marriage academically for 30 years and arranged marriage for eight. He has interviewed 100 couples whose marriages were arranged.

4. He thinks love grows more slowly in an arranged marriage and is therefore, eventually, deeper and more committed than being 'in love' at the beginning which is the basis for marriages which are not arranged. He believes that the planning which goes into an arranged marriage can work better than leaving it to chance – although he says he is not recommending arranged marriage but believes 'a lot can be learnt from them'.

5. She thinks that once a marriage has been arranged it becomes very difficult to get out of so the couple are more committed than they would be if they knew divorce was available as an easy option. There is determination to make it work and if times are hard the difficulties can bring the couple closer together, she argues. She also points out that parents and matchmakers work very hard to make sure that the couple being introduced are compatible and have shared values. She concedes, however, that no marriage will work without some spark – 'chemistry' – between the couple.

6. Journalist, Paul Bentley has described Robert Epstein's published views in a neutral, unbiased way. Then, rather oddly, he adds Francine Kaye's views which echo Epstein's. It might have been stronger if, for balance, he had found someone comparable, such as an author, academic or counsellor, to speak against arranged marriage in an authoritative way. And to be really interesting the piece needs some case studies for human interest – information about, and quotations from, people in arranged marriages. As it is the piece is rather dry.

EXERCISE 10.6

Suggestions only:

1. Once Vicky <u>had sung</u> she curtsied.

2. Ben apologised but he <u>had sworn</u> before. (or he'd)

3. After we <u>had looked</u> at several restaurants we chose the Chinese one. (or we'd)

4. Before you <u>had arrived</u> we started the lesson. (or you'd)

5. I <u>had played</u> tennis before I came to this school. (or I'd)

6. My grandparents <u>had lived</u> in Hampshire all their lives but eventually they moved to a bungalow near us.

EXERCISE 10.7

11. Contractions are words like 'aren't' and 'shouldn't' which are used in this sentence. Both reduce 'not' to 'n't' as we do in speech. More and more writers now use contractions as written styles become less formal. They are still inappropriate in, for example, legal documents or reference books. Some newspapers still use no contractions – *The Stage*, for example.

12. 'No' and the 'not' in 'don't' are both negatives. Logically they cancel each other out. The sentence should read 'Don't use double negatives' or 'Use no double negatives.' In practice many forms of spoken English use double negatives for emphasis ('I ain't got nothing' etc.).

13. Don't use signs such as & (called an ampersand) in your writing and avoid abbreviations which your reader might not be familiar with.

14. The two commas in his sentence are both incorrect.

15. He means 'Never use a big word when a short word will do.' He uses 'diminutive' and 'suffice' to show that long words should be used only when there is no alternative.

16. Exclamation marks are a lazy choice. They make writing look amateurish as this sentence shows. If you choose the right words you don't need them so they can usually be omitted. It is always incorrect to use more than one.

17. He means 'irrespective' or 'regardless'. 'Irregardless' does not exist.

18. There should be no apostrophe in the first 'its' which is possessive. The second 'it's' needs an apostrophe because it's a contraction of 'it is'. Remember that 'its' is a possessive pronoun so it does not take an apostrophe.

19. 'Groan' is a joke. It should read 'grown.' It's witty because when people hear puns – jokes depending on words which sound the same or similar – traditionally they groan because it's a childish form of humour.

20. The words 'have left' are missing.

EXERCISE 10.8

This is not an exhaustive list:

1. Link between two parts, e.g. in woodwork
2. Hinge between bones, e.g. knee
3. Piece of meat
4. Crack in a rock
5. Shady bar or meeting place
6. Illegal cannabis cigarette
7. Shared, e.g. joint account (as an adjective)

EXERCISE 10.9

Here are 21 as a starting point. Pupils will think of more:

dent, died, dies, dine, done, ides, jest, joined, node, nose, note, send, sent, side, sine, site, snide, stone, tide, tine, tone

EXERCISE 10.10

1. compliment – a kind remark or gift (with compliments)
   complement – to complete, finish or add to (complementary colours)
2. councillor – member of a council (e.g. school council)
   counsellor – someone who gives advice or counsel
3. elusive – can't be got hold of because it eludes you or slips out of reach
   illusive – based on illusion so not really there (also illusory)
4. gorilla – large ape
   guerrilla – refers to small unofficial armies (guerrilla warfare)
5. alter – to change
   altar – holy place